TOP SECRET

HOW I GET **PAID** FOR USING

Social Media

Liam William

© **Copyright 2019 - All rights reserved.**

The contents of this book may not be reproduced, duplicated or transmitted without direct written permission from the author.

Legal Notice:

You cannot amend, distribute, sell, use, quote or paraphrase any part or the content within this book without the consent of the author.

Content Table

- **INTRODUCATION**
- **CHAPTER ONE**
- - WHAT IS SOCIAL MEDIA
- - SOCIAL MEDIA AND YOUR BRAND
- **CHAPTER TOW**
- - WHAT WILL I LEARN?
- - SOCIAL MEDIA JOURNEY
- - WHAT IS A TARGET GROUP?
- - SOCIAL MEDIA CHANNELS
- - FOUR TIPS FOR MESSAGING
- - SELECTING AND USING THE RIGHT CONTENT
- - MANAGING YOUR SOCIAL MEDIA PRESENCE
- - THE ROLE OF A SOCIAL MEDIA MANAGER
- - A DAY IN THE LIFE – SOCIAL MEDIA ASSISTANT
- - SOCIAL MEDIA MANAGEMENT TOOLS
- **CHAPTER THREE**
- - USING SOCIAL MEDIA CHANNELS AND MEASURING YOUR SUCCESS
- - HOW TOU USE TWITTER AND INSTAGRAM
- - TWITTER TOP TIPS
- - THE IMPORTANT OF LINKEDIN
- **CHAPTER FOUR**
- - SOCIAL MEDIA TOP TIPS
- - WHY IS PERFORMANCE MEASURMENT IMPORTANT ?
- - SOCIAL MEDIA LISTING
- **CHAPTER FIVE**
- - DECODING A JOB DESCRITION – SOCIAL MEDIA

- - CREATE A SOCIAL MEDIA JOURNEY
- THINGS TO KEEP IN MIND

ABOUT THE AUTHOR

Liam William, who has over 20 years' experience in delivering excellent digital customer experiences to very high profile businesses.

Liam loves working in digital because every day involves talking and thinking about new and exciting ideas which might change the way we live and work! He has particularly enjoyed working in the charity, education and energy industries.

Liam was first interested in starting his career in digital after he designed and coded the first ever BBC Radio 1 website. He then went on to manage the world's first download music chart for MTV and more recently lead a digital agency which advised businesses on their digital strategy. He grew the business from a tiny start-up to a global company spanning the UK, Australia, and Asia.

Liam is really passionate about educating the workforce of tomorrow, especially in digital skills which will be required in almost all jobs in the ever-changing world we live in. He often speaks at events all around the world about digital transformation and customer experience, and regularly comments on digital and business change through his blog and social media channels. In his personal time, Liam loves cooking and getting outdoors with his family, especially with his two energetic little boys.

INTRODUCATION

What is social media?

Today I'm going to be speaking to you about how social media can be used in an effective way for your business. So let's start off by defining what social media is. Social media is tools, websites, and applications. They're all great for sharing, creating, content, videos, ideas, pictures, even your opinions of what you have for breakfast. And you see all these things every day that help you build those networks across the world.

Now all of these things that we use in our everyday life-- I mean Facebook released in 2004, Twitter in 2006, Instagram in 2010, and even Snapchat just more recently-- all of these things, you're using them on a daily basis. But now, it's becoming more and more prevalent to see these networks become established in big business. How can these be relevant for the business world of today? That's what we're going to look at. So let's talk about why big businesses are taking social media so seriously all of a sudden. Well there's an interesting fact.

If you think about the last 60 seconds or so which you've been watching this video, there have been over 276,000 tweets, 246,000 Facebook posts, with 1.8 million likes, and 72 hours of YouTube video uploaded, and about 120 LinkedIn members. Now those are serious insights, serious information, and lots of interesting and impactful insights and data that businesses can make the most use of.

Social media and your brand

What are we going to look at next is talk a little bit about more social media and how exactly you can build your brand using social media and what it gives you in its tools. What is a brand, and what do I mean by a brand? When you're walking down the street, your face is your brand. But online, where you put down in your profiles on your social media, that one little sentence, that one paragraph, that one picture in logo of your company and your business, that is going to become your brand.

So you have to think very carefully exactly what you want to tell to your target audience and the people that are going to be looking at your brand. How does your brand change with the different types of social media that you are going to decide to use? If we think about Facebook, if you would like to take your business on Facebook, it has to be a little bit more dynamic, a little bit more interactive. You have to post a lot of pictures. Try to interact on a daily basis because if you think about the audience that Facebook has, it's

Actually quite a lot of people that will be seeing messages from your company or your business.

And they'll be really thinking about it, so a lot of pictures, a lot of interactive information. If we look at LinkedIn, on the other hand, it's a little bit the more professional side of Facebook. On Facebook, you can have your personal profile and you can have your company profile. Same applies to LinkedIn, but it has to be in a little bit more professional sense.

With LinkedIn, you can create your own page. Your face will be your brand, so you can connect with your colleagues, with other companies.

If you create a piece, a LinkedIn page about your company specific, you can use it in terms of recruitment, in terms of connecting with other companies, in terms of connecting potential people that you want to take on board for your business. So LinkedIn is the bit that needs to be a little bit more professional, a bit more up to the point, a little bit succinct, and telling the most important details and information that you'd like other people, individuals, or other companies to know about your business or yourself.

Now, if we think about all the facts and all the different types of social media that we mention, we have to make a decision in terms of which particular social media you would like to use. You don't need to use all social media altogether. You have to think about which channel is more appropriate for the different target group you would like to reach out to. For example, if you're reaching out to a demographic that is younger, it may be more applicable to use Facebook. If you want to connect with other companies and use them in your own business or recruit, you may want to use LinkedIn.

So we have to really take a moment and think about what is our social media strategy going to be? Which type of social media is it going to be the most useful for us, and it's going to do the most for us? So take a moment. Write down what each social media type can give to you. And then decide what your strategy is going to be, what message you want to carry, and how you want to connect with people.

Week One

In Week one of Social Media we will be covering the following:

Social media journeys
What are target groups?
Social media channels
Tips for messaging
Selecting and using the right content
Managing your social media presence
The role of a social media manager
Social media management tools

What will I learn?

Describe what social media is
Explain why social media is relevant for businesses
Describe the role that social media can play in building or enhancing your brand
Explain the importance of having a social media strategy

By the end of this chapter you will be able to:
Explain the key steps for a brand in their social media journey
Describe the importance of setting objectives
Explain why it is important to identify and understand your target audience and select your social media channels based on this
Outline what aspects should be considered when creating messaging for social channels
Explain how to get started managing your social media presence

Social media journey

Let's explain the five key things a business needs to consider in order to use social media effectively.

Your journey to creating a social media presence involves:

Setting your objectives

Choosing your target audience

Selecting the social media channels you will use

Creating your messaging

Managing your social media presence

Our social media journey in this book is going to have five stops. The first stop is objectives - if you look from your perspective as a business, the things you have on your agenda, the things that you would like to achieve as a business and the directions you would like to go into, how can you use social media to achieve them? Our second stop will be target groups. What that means is how can you reach out to the different target groups that you have identified for your businesses using social media tools that are available to you? Our third stop is channels.

So if you think about from the perspective of your business, once you have identified your objectives, your target group, what kind of social media channels are you going to use to reach out to them? Are you going to use one particular social media channel or are you going to use multiple? And how, in what correlation are you going to use them? So stop number three - channels. Step number four is messaging. What do I mean by messaging? If you think about what you want to tell to the world and your customers and everyone who'd like to hear about your company, what message do you want to tell them?

What message do you want to communicate with the social media tools that you're going to have at your disposal? The fifth stop of our social media journey, which is also one of the most important ones, is managing. If you think about all the social media tools that you have at your disposal and all the information that's going around the world every 60 seconds, huge quantities of information, managing is key. How would you like to manage information and the message you're giving away ? What kind of frequency are you going to use? Are you going to put post every hour, are you going to post every couple of hours or every day ? Or what kind of tools are you going to use ?

So all the messages that you want to give out to people and other businesses and the audience that you're going to have, you have to carefully manage. You have to have a strategy in terms of managing. There are various tools that are social media tailored; you can use to manage your messages for all the different kinds of social media networks and tools that you're going to use. So think about managing - how would you like to manage your message? What would you like to do? What's going to make it easier for you to carry the message out to your audiences?

What is a target group?

In this book you will learn why it is important to understand your target group in order to deliver the right product or message, and to choose the best channel to connect with them.

Think about three different target audiences:
College students
Young professionals
Women aged 40+

So once again, setting objectives is absolutely important. The reason being that once you've got these great objectives, they'll really help you with the following steps. So when it comes to defining your target audience , it would be much simpler to pick the right demographics and after that, actually figure out the right channels and the right messages that you want to get out to them. And the definition of a target group is really the intended audience that you want to deliver your product to. Who are you actually focusing your message towards? And who are they? And actually to define that, I like to expand on that and say, it's all about figuring out who that person is.

What kind of personality they have. What do they like to drink? What do they do on the weekends? What kind of shoes do they wear? Where do they go to hang out? What restaurants do they eat at? The more you understand about that individual, that target group, the more you're able to tailor your message and your product. So let's take an example that we gave earlier. If you look at the example of a concert - you've got a music concert. Think about the type of artist that you want to invite that your target group would like to come and watch. So think about the people that you're looking at. What kind of music are they into?

What kind of talent do they support? Who do they follow on Twitter? Who do they follow on Facebook? You have to make sure that the product that you're delivering is right for that target group. So understanding their likes, their dislikes and also their brand associations. What I mean by that is what other brands do they like? Are those brands going to be present there? Can you have a network with them? Understanding more about your customer, your consumer, your client allows you to deliver a better product. So let's take a look at an earlier example I gave about the clothing brand. And let's say that you've got a fantastic sports clothing product that you're really, really proud of.

It's now about identifying the right target group to deliver it to. Understanding what your target group value is extremely important. And seeing as you're a sports brand, some of things are probably fitness, health, and well-being. And you want to be able to deliver your message around those core values, so that your target group can relate to you and relate to your brand and product. If they feel that it ticks these three boxes for them, they're more likely to go out and buy it from you. Identifying your target group is an extremely important activity. The better you understand these individuals, the better you'll be able to do the next step, which is selecting the channels that you want to market through. Understanding your target group means you know which channels they're using more - which ones do they use, when do they use them, and how they use them. So once you've

Done that, we can then move on to identifying the networks and channels to market and get your message across. So let's take a look at a real life example of how a brand has actually changed its strategy and approach due to the rise of social media. One of the

An example that strikes in my mind is actually from last Christmas. And every Christmas, there's always a fantastic advert that comes out. It's usually by John Lewis.
And last year, the star of their advert was Monty the Penguin, and I'm sure you've seen it. And it was hash tag Monty the Penguin

across social media. And in the past couple of years, it's been the first time that John Lewis has actually chosen to go out on social media, including YouTube, Facebook, and Twitter. And the amount of views that they had in a couple of days was absolutely outstanding, absolutely successful campaign. And the reason why it happened is because they understood that their target group that may have originally been watching television, actually now has actually started using YouTube and Facebook and Twitter much, much more.

Now that we've identified your target group, it's important to figure out which channels we're going to use to communicate your message. What we mean by channels is the various networks at your disposal that you can use to communicate that message, the mediums that are available to you to actually get your message out there, your brand out there, and talk to those individuals to actually build that conversation. It's important to know that actually different channels are right for different target groups. Originally, when we're speaking about that objective, it's important to understand how we're going to achieve it through the channels and the target groups actually matching up with each other.

We know that, for example, that if you were going to try and recruit or build a professional brand, you'd tend to LinkedIn instead of Facebook. However, if you were trying to promote a new concert or maybe looking at that clothing brand or that clothing line again, then, of course, Instagram, those visual messages or video on

Facebook and YouTube are going to come to the forefront. So this is the way we start to understand which networks work for which audience.

Social Media channels

Learn about a few popular social media channels and the type of content that is most appropriate to post or share on each of them.

This rule states that your audience will decide whether or not they are interested in the first 8 seconds! This is why it is so important to make sure your content grabs the attention of your audience immediately.

So Facebook lets you communicate your message through so many different mediums. But other channels, other networks, are actually a bit more niche, a bit more specific. So let's take a look at Twitter, for example. Twitter's fantastic to get a trend going. You want to be trending in your town, trending in your city, trending in your country. And I mean trending globally would be fantastic. The way you do that is by monitoring the hash tags, actually following the right hash tags, sharing with the right hash tags, and sharing around key times in the world. Let's take a quick look at Instagram. Instagram works quite similarly, but, obviously, this time with images. You want images that are striking. You want images that stand out.

You want images that people can immediately connect to. The best images on Instagram are ones that prompt a bit of humor, something a little funny, something a bit different. Something a bit quirky, that gets everyone laughing and talking about it.

Remember, you can never make anything go viral. You can only see it go viral when it's actually happened. Another one that we'll want to look at is YouTube. Like I said about the eight second rule with Facebook, YouTube, of course, gives you a bit longer. But you still want to focus on two to three minute videos at best to get your message across in the right way.

Four tips for messaging

When developing content you should keep a few things in mind to ensure your message has the impact that you want it to have. Watch this video to learn about the following top tips:

Defining the subject and topic
Determining whether it is relevant

Defining the style
Assessing the strength of the content

Now that we've identified the channel and networks, it's really time that we start to focus on defining and creating our message.
At the end of the day, that content is going to be king on these channels, the content that people see, the content that people read, the content that you want people to experience, that's what we're going to focus on now. And we've got four tips for you that we're going to focus on.
The first one is looking at defining the subject and topic.
The second one is taking a look at whether it's relevant in the current landscape or what's happening in the world today.

The third is defining the style, getting that style spot on, a method of communicating.

And finally, actually assessing and defining the strength. Is that content piece strong? Do other people like it? So now that we've identified your subject and theme, it's really important to see whether that's actually topical.
Is there some event that's just happened in the world that it relates to? Has something just happened in your city that it connects to?

Are there any way that you can look at those trends that are happening in the world of business or fashion, or whatever industry that you're working in, and see if you can use those as ways to amplify your brand and product?

So now that we've identified your subject and theme, we've confirmed that it's topical, it's really important to take a look at the style of the messaging. It's really important to think about how do we want this to be communicated? Do we want the message to be promotional?
Or do we want it to be persuasive? Or do we want it to be informative? Understanding what experience you want to people looking at it to have will help you define that message. Understanding what response you want , will help you to communicate it in the right way. The fourth step you want to take is what we call a review.

We want to actually take a look at that piece of content you've produced and say is it best as a picture? Is it best as a video? Or is it best as a statistic or a question? Doing this helps you actually pick the right medium in which to communicate that message.

Selecting and using the right content

This chapter explains why different message formats are useful for different purposes, and how your choice of format will affect how your audience interacts with your content.

Alongside creating and defining your message, it's really important to think about the format in which it will be delivered. It's also really important to take into consideration

How your audience will actually interact with that message. We're going to take a look at these two extra aspects right now. There are several different formats of communicating a message. You've got text, audio, image, and video. When we start looking at these a bit more in-depth, let's start off with text. Of course, when you're sending a tweet, you've got 140 characters. Those letters become extremely precious. But if you're writing a blog, you may have 500 to 1,000 words.

Understanding whether your audience is going to consume that information while they're travelling or while they're actually at work or whether they're doing it in their social time will help you to frame that message effectively . If you want people to grab things while they're on lunch, tweet is probably the best avenue of 140 characters being used wisely. If you want to actually communicate a big report, or maybe a new research study, then actually that blog may be best suited. The next one I want to look at is audio. Now audio, these days, is most prevalent or famous in terms of podcast. If your audience is going to consume this while they commute into work or maybe just before they go to bed well, or maybe the first thing when they wake up in the morning, it may even be while they're at the gym. The point is they'll be doing another activity while they consume this audio information. So think about when are your audience actually going to be using this or interacting with it? If it's a time when they're usually going to be doing something else, audio's the one for that. The third one I want to take a look at is video.

Video is a fantastic form of communication if you want people to feel an experience, if you want them to engage with an emotion, if you want to tell a story, if you want to take people on a journey with you, you want to use a video. Now remember, it's important to note that video shouldn't be too long. So you're looking at 30 seconds to two minutes to really have an impactful view on your audience, to really get that effect across. And the final one I want to touch on is image. Images are great for grabbing instant moments.

Whether it's happiness, whether it's an emotion, whether it's a great new finding, or whether you just met a celebrity, those moments are best captured by a picture. So making sure that those pictures are taken to the right quality is also very important. If your brand is quite edgy and attracting a younger audience, you may want those pictures actually not

To be HD quality. You may want to take them on your iPhone. But actually, if you're trying to put them into a nice website, a professional LinkedIn portfolio, or something of that sort, you want to make sure you've got that quality right. Previously we looked at the format of your content and how that will be delivered.
It's also important now to take a look at how it's actually going to be accessed and interacted with by your audience. From your audience's point of view, there are three key important things for them. The first one is accessibility. Can they access the information in the place and the time that they want to? For example, if you're expecting them to access it at work, do they have portals that block any of these access points? Making sure that the access point is open to your target audience is extremely important. The second thing to look at is whether your audience can actually interact with the information and interact with your content. Do you want them to be able to comment on it?
Do you want them to be able to like it? Do you want them to be able to tag other people in it? When you show them this content, it's

extremely important to remember what's right for your audience and right for your brand. There are certain YouTube videos that, for example, block comments. Some of them leave it open to all. Just another important consideration. The settings you place in your content are extremely important. Whether it's shared across one network or three networks, it's important that you clarify this and categories this well. There's just two other things that I want you to remember - property rights and privacy.

IN terms of property rights, I want you to think can you actually share that content? Do you need to source it? Do you need to ask for permission? Is that content original and does it belong to you? It's really, really important to make sure that that content is certified to be shared under your brand name and in terms of your products. The second thing is privacy. Are you sharing any sensitive information, any confidential information about your clients, your customers, or your business that actually is not for viewing for the extended audience? Make sure that the privacy settings are correct in this area because any mistakes will actually cause a lot of trouble for you and your business.

Managing your social media presence

Let's take a look at the importance of managing your social media channels and 3 things to do in order to manage this effectively:
Decide who will be responsible for day to day management
Decide when updates will be made
Analyze to check if objectives are being met

So we've now been through all the challenging steps of actually developing a campaign. We're now at the stage where we have to think about how it should run day-to-day, what are the things that are going to pop up on a daily basis, and how are we going to make sure that we manage the whole lifeline of this campaign effectively? There are three things we're going to look at in this area. The first thing is actually looking at who should be responsible for managing the campaign on a daily basis. It's a really important role. The second thing is looking at when are we going to do these updates? How often are we going to do them?
And who's actually going to make sure that those things happen? And the third thing is to actually monitor, to analyze, to listen closely, to match our progress and make sure we're reaching our objectives, or make changes at the right time. So let's take a look at them now.

The role of a social media manager

Will go into more detail about how to manage a social media campaign effectively.

Let's to learn about what makes a good social media manager, some key considerations, and more!

So let's now take a look at the role of a social media manager. The social media manager has to be someone who's extremely familiar with all the networks. They need to know the ins and outs and the tips and the tricks so that when it comes to it, they know how to manage any changes or any responses effectively. One of the key things about the social media manager is that they have to be dedicated to this full-time. Hopefully, as soon as you post something, you'd have responses from that minute throughout the whole day. It's important that you interact with your audience and actually reciprocate with their messages, and their thoughts, and comments.

People often ask the question how often I should post on a social network. Will people get bored of me? Is that too much? Well actually all the different networks have different post rates that actually work for them. You see with the LinkedIn blog post, usually once a week to receive a good piece of thought leadership is acceptable. It's a business level 500 to 1000 word documents, and therefore it requires time to consume. However, if you look at YouTube, with 72 hours uploaded in only a minute, you can see that the rate of YouTube uploading can be much, much faster.

Now you want to be able to stagger your content across YouTube as well so you get the most out of it. Once again, once a week works extremely well. It helps people get into the guessing game and wanting to see your next video. However, now if you look in the other networks of Facebook, Instagram, or Twitter, you're looking at multiple times per day. The reason is people check those networks multiple times per day. If they're going on it more often, they need to be interacting with your content every time they go on as a touch point, as a checkpoint.

So what I'd recommend from that is Facebook, you could have five a day, Twitter, a minimum five a day, and Instagram, five a day as well as a minimum. All of these will make sure that your presence is consistent, and that people are interacting with you

Whenever they sign on. We're now going to look at how we're going to monitor the impact of your post, the impact of your message. It's extremely important to remember that all of

These posts, the whole journey we've been through, were to achieve specific objectives that we set at the very beginning. Cross analyzing your posts and the objectives that you set originally is extremely important.

Making sure that you're ticking those objectives, maybe even surpassing them, would be a fantastic way to start monitoring. The second thing we need to look at is actually analyzing trends and patterns that will help us define the strategy for the next five days, the five weeks, or the next five months. One of the insights that we're gaining from how we're seeing our audience interact with what we're producing. Are they commenting more in certain posts? Do they like other posts more? Are they sharing particular formats more than others? Becoming more aware of all these things will help you get the right format out in the future and help you define and design amazing content.

A Day in The Life – Social Media Assistant

We talked about the role of a Social Media Manager in the last step. Now, let's have a closer look at an entry-level role, and what a typical day in this job might look like for a Social Media Assistant. Have a look at the info graphic below to get an idea of a typical day of a Social Media Assistant.

A DAY IN THE LIFE OF...
A SOCIAL MEDIA ASSISTANT

What is work in Social Media like?

If you work in Social Media, you will help to promote or represent a company on Social Media platforms to increase awareness and customer engagement.

As a Social Media Assistant, you can expect to create content for different platforms, monitor people's engagement, respond as necessary, and analyse how well previous posts have been received or what kind of content works best.

You will probably work together with a Social Media manager and help them to implement the company's Social Media marketing strategy.

As a junior Social Media professional, your entry level salary is likely to start at £18 - 23,000 a year, and rise to between £25 - 40,000 after 3-5 years in the job. These figures vary depending on your location and industry.

What are some of the key skills that you'd develop in this job?

 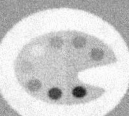   

Writing and copy-editing	Boldness & Creativity	No fear of numbers	Interest in digital & networks	Communication
You will likely write copy yourself or proofread what others have written.	In social media you have only seconds to attract attention - creating interesting hooks is key.	You will do some analysis of data to find out what works and what doesn't.	You'll want to stay on top of trends, new networks and successful campaigns.	In the end, it's all about getting your message across - in person, in writing and via multiple media.

What are the tools of the trade?

Social Media networks | **Social Media Listening and Monitoring tools** | **Social Media Scheduling tools** | **Image editing software**

You will spend a lot of time on Social Media platforms like Twitter, Facebook, Instagram or LinkedIn.

Many have built-in (also often called "native") analysis and planning tools as well.

These tools help you to identify and assess what is being said about a brand on the Internet.

This helps to see how popular a brand is - and alerts you to negative comments.

Publishing the right content at the right time to the right channel requires good planning.

Social Media management and scheduling tools can help you do that.

Social Media is full of images.

Learning to work with image editing software means you can edit your own visual content to go with your posts.

A typical day

9am

The first thing you do in the morning is check your emails, as well as all the Social Media pages your company is active on. You assess reactions to recent posts, levels of engagement, and notifications - and ensure that none of your posts have backfired.

You also take the time to respond to customer questions where they come up.

In the world of Social Media, it's important to stay on top of what's going on, and you often have to react quickly.

10am

You catch up with your manager to confirm the priorities for the day.

Together, you check the content plan you created previously, and confirm that all the scheduled posts are good to go.

A content plan is a plan of posts, tweets and uploads that will happen during a certain period - usually a week or a month.

10:30am

You spend the rest of the morning with an analysis of the current paid advertisement campaign on Facebook.

Where you pay for content on social media, you want to make sure it is effective. You can look at the number of likes, shares, clicks and conversions, which means the number of people buying a product or signing up because of the advert.

You notice that one of the adverts isn't performing well, so you check with your manager before making adjustments to it.

12pm

Lunchtime!
You check your Social Media accounts - you're following a few Social Media experts, and it's always interesting to see what they are getting up to.

Maybe you also check for news about your industry, or you see if there's anything interesting on one of the blogs you're following.

1pm

You need to create a new content plan for next week. But first you double check what content worked best in the last week.

You look at the "organic" posts from last week - that's the posts that are not paid advertising - and check which ones got many likes and shares, and which ones didn't.

What do the good ones have in common? Are they more emotional or informative? What kind of images and hashtags do they use?

2pm

You already know the topics of the posts for next week - now you have to write them!

Keeping the findings from the analysis you just did in mind, you create some compelling content in different formats for the different Social Media channels: for example beautiful images for Instagram, a short headline and an effective hashtag for Twitter or a professional blog post for LinkedIn.

4pm

You have a meeting with your manager to go through the content and sign it off.

Your manager will pay attention to the tone of the post to ensure it's targeting the right audience and is aligned to your company's overall brand.

It's interesting to learn from their experience and discuss what works and what doesn't!

5pm

Every once in a while, you go to an event and cover it live on Twitter. Today, you are going to the opening of a new store - some famous people are expected!

Your job is to tweet about what's going on and share photos of the new shop and the guests.

Before the event, you created a hashtag with your team that you will be using. You will also include this hashtag on any marketing materials for the new shop to drive engagement and to be able to monitor conversations around the topic.

Don't get put off by the jargon!

Engagement rate	The percentage of people who interact with a particular piece of content. The engagement rate takes into account factors such as number of likes, comments and shares.
Key Performance Indicator (KPI)	A key performance indicator (KPI) is a measurable value that helps evaluate progress towards a goal. For example, a KPI for measuring the success of a Social Media campaign may include the number of likes, shares or mentions that the campaign receives.
Social Listening	Monitoring digital conversations to understand what is being said about a brand, industry or specific topic. For example, a company could use social listening to understand what their customers are saying about them on Social Media channels. The feedback from social listening can help a company to differentiate their brand or service, and create content tailored for those audiences.
Social Media channels	The means, networks or platforms used to interact and communicate with people. Examples of Social Media channels include Facebook, Twitter, Snapchat and LinkedIn. Can also be referred to as 'channel'.

Social media management tools

Managing a social media campaign across multiple channels can be difficult, so this chapter introduces you to some tools that can help you manage your campaign, and analyze how your audience are engaging with your content.

In your role as a social media manager, it's really important that you pick the right tools to work with. The reason is because you don't want to be going onto each and every network to post the same content or having to go to each network to respond. There's some fantastic management tools out there like Hoot Suite or Sprout Social and several different ones that will be coming up in the future. And all of these tools have some really key features. The first thing is that they let you manage your networks from one place. It means from one place, you can work across Facebook, Twitter, LinkedIn, Instagram, and even Interest. Another key feature is that you can actually schedule your posts.

You don't have to be there at 9:00 AM every day doing them away on the actual day of posting. You could schedule a week in advance, a month in advance, or as far in advance as you like to make your job simpler. Another key feature is that a lot of these have simple analytics built in. You can immediately see the rate at which your posts are growing or the rate at which they're shared. These management tools make your process and your life really, really simple, and some of them are even free. So use them and give them a go. Everything we've discussed here about managing your social media presence can be contextualized with three simple words, listen, engage, and monitor.

So when we listen, we understand what our target group really wants. We engage with them in a conversation, engage and interact with our content, and actually getting that message across. We then monitor and use those analytics to optimize what we do in the future. Taking a look at a real world example, we take a look at Ford fiestas. When they had their new launch, Ford selected 100 individuals that they believed were very

Influential in social media. These people naturally, pre-launch, started to write about it, tweet about it, blog about it. And they found that the 700 videos that were actually uploaded gathered 6.5 million views.

And from that, they had hundreds and thousands of people actually asking about Ford from which most of them were non-Ford customers. It's an amazing impact an amazing story to show how influential people on social media made all the difference.

WEEK TOW

USING SOCIAL MEDIA CHANNELS AND MEASURING YOUR SUCCESS

Top tips for using social media channels

We will explore some examples of different social media channels and some top tips for getting started in social media for your business.

What will I learn?

In this chapter, we'll be giving you some top tips for using social media channels.

By the end of this chapter you will be able to:

List examples of different social media channels and the features available on these channels

Explain the importance of LinkedIn for businesses and individuals

List some top tips for using Twitter and LinkedIn effectively

Explain how to use social media in a professional or work context

How to use Twitter and Instagram

Now will learn more about Twitter and Instagram, the benefits of using them, and what types of content to post on each of these channels to use them effectively.

How can Twitter and Instagram be used to promote a business you're interested in or admire?

Note: Twitter now allows 280 characters instead of the former 140

If we now put a little bit more context around social media and pick two particular types of social media, which are Twitter and Instagram, what can you do with them? What do they give you? If we take Twitter for example, less is more. You have 140 characters to tell exactly what you want to say. And if you pitch the right message with the right words, using the right hash tags and the right mentions or the "@" symbol, you're going to reach an incredibly huge audience of people, and you're going to make an impact.

To put that into perspective and give you a little bit of a personal example, not too long ago, I was reading a business book and I really, really enjoyed it, so I just wanted to express my enjoyment with the book on Twitter using social media. So I wrote a Twitter post using 140 characters, and I tweeted to the author, mentioning his name, using the hash tag for the title of the book. And I said, I really enjoyed that book. Thank you very much. And two hours later, to my surprise, the author actually tweeted back to me.

He said he was really pleased that I enjoyed his work, and he said, let's take it to email and email a little bit so that I learn exactly what you enjoyed about the book. So I thought that was absolutely amazing because if you think about it, two years ago, you would not have had a chance to engage with authors, with celebrities, with people that are outside of your immediate network. Twitter connects you with the world. It connects you right now, right this second, and you can get immediate responses from people that are across the world.

So for your business, this can be incredibly powerful because if you create your own profile on Twitter, if you connect with people that you like, people that you like to follow, if you write the right messages using the appropriate hash tags, the appropriate mentions,

You can expand your network millions of times. And you can grow incredibly fast. So just think about exactly what you want to say on Twitter. On Instagram, on the other hand, you can share pictures. And you can add a little caption to the picture, but the picture actually carries the message. So you know when they say that a picture is worth a thousand words, well, that is exactly what Instagram does for you.

So nowadays a lot more brands and businesses are actually going first to Instagram than any other social media to post their pictures, their products, information about the company in a very, very cool and creative way. And they reach a very huge audience because nowadays, all the young people, the young generation, they all have Instagram. That's how they communicate with each other. One very cool feature of Instagram is that you can actually make a video and post it. So you not only have shared pictures, you can make it a little bit more dynamic. So think about the picture content, the visuals that you would like to share with your audience, and do it via Instagram.

Twitter top tips

Start to use Twitter more effectively by following these three tips:

Engage and follow

Interact

Listen and manage

To give you something more tangible to go away after the end of this module, would be my three tips for Twitter. So the first one would be engage with people, follow people, follow people that you know, also follow people that may be of interest to you or may be in the same line of business or may be in the same line of interesting topics. Second tip would be engage rather than broadcast. Nowadays you can get showered by messages from different a company which almost to us feels like spam, and it's rather broadcasting.

But to make your engagement on Twitter and your presence on Twitter more meaningful and more interactive and actually more useful for yourself and your company or your brand or your business, engage with people. That's going to drive conversations. That is going to drive hash tags. That is going to drive actually engagement with people outside of your network. The third top tip will be listening, manage, and analyze. What I mean by listen in the social media context is actually look at the different hash tags that are going around, look at what your connections are posting, and look at what is the general topic. Google hash tags if you like and then participate in the conversations. This way you're going to become more visible.

People are going to see your name. They're going to see your Twitter handle. And if what you're saying is actually interesting to them, they're going to follow you. So content, and listening, and engaging in the right way is very key. Managing and then analyzing is just for you to take away all these messages that are coming your way and finding the right way to actually engage in the conversations and become part of the trends.

The importance of LinkedIn

In this chapter you will learn about the importance of having a presence on LinkedIn, for both individuals and businesses, and how you can use LinkedIn to expand your professional network.

If we're going to explore another social media network that is a little bit more professional, let's look into LinkedIn. So nowadays, there are about 360 million professionals worldwide who have LinkedIn profiles. That is one incredible network of people that you can actually get connected to and leverage by just creating a profile. If you think about it, if you don't have a LinkedIn profile, if you don't have a picture on your LinkedIn profile or a picture of your brand or your logo or description, you're almost invisible to those 360 million people. So LinkedIn is able to create amazing things about your brand.

If you have the right message there, if you have your brand logo, your ideas, your mission, vision statement, anything that you would like to put there, you can actually add similar businesses. You can recruit. You can add potential clients. You can add your clients, your current clients. And one very interesting fact is that if you have new clients or clients are considering doing business with you, inevitably they're going to go on your LinkedIn page and check your history, your previous work. So therefore, it's very, very important to be visible, to create your brand, to create your face on LinkedIn, be there, engage with different groups, add people, exchange ideas, post various things on LinkedIn.

This is actually a feature that's not used that well these days. You can create blogs. You can post about your ideas. You can talk about trends. You can talk about things that your company is working on , your business is working on, your ideas. So LinkedIn can expand your professional network immensely, so do leverage that, do leverage those 360 million people. Be there and be visible.

Social media top tips

Finally, we've got three tips that can help you use social media effectively:

Observe and learn

Explore new ideas (whilst remembering best practices)

Use new channels and tools

Now I'm going to share with you my top three tips for social media. My first one is observe and learn from the people that use it best. Look at those influences, look at those leaders online, see how they use social media channels, see how they interact on those networks, and emulate them. Don't copy them, but just try and learn and observe those tips and tricks. My second one is really use social media as a personal experiment, of course, within everything we've said before. But definitely try and be open to exploring new ideas, new content trying and be a bit quirky, try out new things.

If you see a new image or a new video style, try and create something with that and share it, because you never know what's going to go viral. And the third thing I'd like to recommend is making sure that if any new network any new tool or any new social media channel is released, make sure you use it. You'll only be able to use a network for business if you've been a consumer. If you used it from that perspective, it can become extremely, extremely powerful. So really be open and try out the new networks. A few things I'd like you to remember as well is that make sure that you always, always remain authentic.

You want to have the right voice, you want to come across original, and you want to be yourself. The second thing I'd like you to remember is actually that in this process, with finding great content, creating and designing new content, you can start to get lost in that process and forget your original objectives. It's really important to always measure and check things against those original objectives you set as a team or for yourself. Good luck and all the best.

Remember, it is important to be authentic and stick to your objectives.

What will I learn?

In this chapter, we will be focusing on how you can measure the success of your social media campaign and improve it by listening to your audience.

By the end of this activity you will be able to:

Explain the importance of measuring your performance on social media

Identify what a key performance indicator (KPI) is

Explain the importance of social media listening

Why is performance measurement important?

Learn what a key performance indicator (KPI) is, and how you can apply this concept to measure the success of your social media campaign.

In this video, we're going to cover why it's important to measure your performance online, what a key performance indicator is, and how you can use these KPIs to measure your success online. As we covered in lesson two, it's really important to set objectives for your brand on social media if you want to get the most out of social media for your business. This is why performance measurement is important, because it's with performance measurement that you can see whether or not you're meeting your objectives. If you're not meeting your objectives, performance measurement lets you know that you need to alter your social media strategy. If you are meeting your objectives, it lets you know that you're on the right track.

It's also important from a financial perspective, because it lets you know where you should be focusing your paid efforts. The most effective way to measure your performance online is to identify and measure your key performance indicators or KPIs. A KPI is a metric or a way of measuring success in a certain area. Let's look at an example from outside of social media. If we think about the Olympic games, the KPI which we would look at in the 100-meter sprint is speed, because speed is what we look at when we think about success in this event.

IN social media, a KPI is anything quantifiable, such as follower count, which is the number of people who are following your brand on a social media channel, or engagement rate, which is the percentage of an audience to engage with a piece of content that they see. If your brand uses social media, you might want to grow your follower community. Here, the KPI would be fan growth. Alternatively, you might want to make sure that a message from your brand reaches as many people as possible. Here, the KPI would be reach. The KPIs which are most relevant to your business will vary depending on what business objectives you're trying to achieve with social media. So how can we measure KPIs?

A great way to do this is to use some of the social media management tools which are out there. These tools can produce reports which show you how your posts and campaigns are doing. They can show you a lot of stuff, but some of the things which they can show you are the time of day that people are engaging with your content, the number of new followers that you're most engaging pieces of content are bringing in, and the engagement rate on your posts. We can use these KPI to make important decisions about the style of content that you want to put out and the tone of your campaigns.

For example, if we think about the KPI of the number of shares on a post, we can compare this KPI between two campaigns to decide which campaign has the most successful tone and style of content. And we can use this information to make decisions about future campaigns. It's important that you're consistently checking your performance against your KPIs as part of your broader social media strategy.

Social Media Listening

Now will explain what social listening is, the useful data it can provide, and how listening to what people say online can be used to improve your social media campaign.

We are going to talk about social listening and how you can use it to measure and improve your performance in social media. Let's define what social listening is. Social listening is monitoring what people are actually saying about your brand, both to the brand and to each other. We can use social listening to get a more holistic view of how people are responding to your content beyond what is revealed in follower counts and engagement rates. What are people actually saying about your brand? What discussions are they having? We can also use social listening to get important information about the people who are having these discussions. Are they your target audience?

What are their demographics, location, and other key attributes? Let's move on to how you can use social listening for your brand. A great way to do this is to utilize the tools which you use for managing your social media. A lot of these tools have an ability to search for keywords, such as your brand name or hash tags which you have developed. By searching for these keywords and tracking them, you can see what kind of buzz is being generated around your posts and around your campaigns. As well as giving you another angle through which to see how people are responding to your content, social listening provides you with another opportunity to engage with your followers.

IN social media, it's important that you talk with your followers and not at them. If you come across something positive which your followers are saying about your brand, it might be appropriate to thank them.

Alternatively, if you come across something negative, you might want to think about how best to respond in order to ensure that your brand maintains a good reputation online. So to wrap up,

Social listening enables you to check how people are responding to your brand online as part of your performance measurement.
The key information which social listening enables you to find out about the people who are having discussions about your brand enables you to make important decisions about how to improve and promote your brand.

Decoding a Job description – Social Media

In case you are planning to apply for a job in the field, have a look at the below example of a job advert decoded.

It can help you to understand how to effectively read job descriptions and what to look out for to help you write the best application possible. On the left-hand side, you can see the advert, and on the right-hand side, you can see some hints about what to look out for when applying.

Decoding a job description

A typical job description | Think about...

Social Media Assistant

It's an 'assistant' position, so likely to be entry-level!

We are a large Social Media agency, and we are looking for an enthusiastic Social Media Assistant to join our growing team. If you love Twitter, Instagram & Co, this could be the perfect opportunity for you to gain experience in developing effective Social Media strategies for our client base.

Key responsibilities | What does this mean?

1. Source and curate imagery

1. Source and curate imagery
Sourcing images means finding or creating them, and curating means selecting images that are relevant to a specific topic and assembling them into a collection (e.g. an interesting Instagram story).

! You could give examples of when you've created or curated content for a blog, newspaper, newsletter etc. are very relevant.

2. Create, schedule and post social media and blog content, including occasional copywriting for our blog

2. Create, schedule and post content
This involves creating written or photo/ video content and developing a plan as to what to publish when in order to best reach the target audience

! Prove that you understand the differences between Social Media platforms and what content works best for each. Also ensure your own Social Media profiles are set to private, or appropriate to be seen by an employer.

3. Keep clear and concise records for each campaign **and compile analytics**. Based on these findings, create weekly and monthly reports

3. Keep clear records & compile analytics
The purpose is to identify what worked well and what didn't so that you can learn from it for the future and improve the effectiveness of campaigns.

! Good to mention experience with analysing data and drawing conclusions from it, or examples of when you've kept a record over time (e.g. for budgeting).

Manage monthly planning documents

4. Manage planning documents
This could involve keeping project plans up to date, requesting updates from team members, updating your manager about progress or alerting them to when things aren't going to plan.

You could highlight experience that involved paying attention to detail or successfully juggling different projects or activities at once.

5. Conduct research related to new media, Social Media strategies, top influencers, competitors and trends in the industry, and stay abreast of the social media landscape

5. Conduct research
Influencers are people who have influence over the target audience your company wants to reach, so it's important to know them - if they share or endorse your content, this could be great advertisement!

Provide examples of your experience with research, and what you do to find out about industry news. For an interview, be prepared to talk about a recent trend you've observed.

Key Skills

What's a good example?

6. Attention to detail, experience of organising own workload, and keeping to deadline

6. Attention to detail & organisation experience
Mention examples of when you've managed several projects or activities at once and describe how you organised your workload. Ensure to spell check and proofread your application to prove attention to detail.

7. Knowledge and understanding of Social Media channels Facebook, Instagram, Twitter, Pinterest, YouTube and Snapchat

7. Knowledge of Social Media channels
If you have large numbers of followers or have ever used Social Media to successfully promote something, those are great examples. Otherwise, you could for example demonstrate your knowledge and interest by analysing one of your future employer's Social Media campaigns.

8. Good communication skills – written, over the phone and in person

8. Communication skills
This also involves the ability to recognise varied audiences and communicate with them in an appropriate manner. Mention examples of when you've targeted a message to a specific audience, held presentations or written something for a wider audience, such as a newspaper article, blog or report.

9. Interest in copywriting

9. Interest in copywriting
Copywriting means producing written content, often for the purpose of marketing. Mention experience of writing content or promoting something - e.g. a fundraising activity, or an event.

10. Skilled with Microsoft Office Suite

10. Skilled with Microsoft Office Suite
This includes MS Excel, PowerPoint and Word. Consider what you'll be likely to use these for: Excel for tracking progress against plans or analysing data such as numbers of followers over time; Word for creating reports or to to write content drafts; PowerPoint to present reports to your managers or others. Mention examples of these experiences and skills.

Create a social media journey

Now you've completed all chapters, you have the opportunity to complete a short writing assignment to share with your peers. It is a great chance to put into practice the things you've learned and get some helpful feedback.

Instructions:

In this activity we have learned about using social media in a business context and the steps that make up the social media journey. This assignment will help you to define your social media purpose and objectives, and target specific audiences or groups of people.

Answer the questions below :

Setting your objectives - Create an example goal, or objective, that you would like to achieve by using social media to promote your brand.
Defining your target audience - Who is your target audience? How could you segment this audience?

Selecting your social media channels - Based on your answers to questions 1 and 2, which social media channels are best for you to use?

Creating content - What content will you share on social media? Think about the topic or theme of the content you will post, and the formats you could use.

Managing your presence - What key performance indicators (KPIs) would you want to measure if you were going to roll out a campaign to your target audience?

Things to keep in mind:

Try to answer all of the questions.

You should aim to spend around 30 minutes completing your assignment and write up to 500 words in total.

Include numbers when you type your answer so that it is clear which question you are answering.

Career Journey – Social Media

If you are wondering what you could do next to build up your social media skillset, we have got you covered. Have a look at the below ideas to get some inspiration for where you could go from here to build up a career in Social Media.

Career Journey
SOCIAL MEDIA

First of all, every career is different and unique.

There are some key steps you can take though that will help you get to where you want to be.

Remember, your career is a journey, and you have to tackle it step by step. You may not be a Manager tomorrow - but the way there is fun and worthwhile!

Here you'll find a few ideas to get you started.

Find Out More!

Podcasts

Podcasts are a great way to learn about new developments, stay up to date with the latest Social Media trends, and hear from influential leaders in the field.

Blogs

Blogs are great sources of information and points of view on key Social Media topics - you can even get involved in the discussion over social media!

Professional Websites

Professional websites showcase exemplary work within the Social Media field and publish articles on best practice for the industry.

Build A Network

Professional networking sites

Follow influencers and interest groups to help you research the industry, and connect with your past and present colleagues to build your network via pages like LinkedIn. You can also try to reach out to other Social Media professionals directly to find out about their career.

Career Fairs or Networking events

Most cities, schools and colleges host careers fairs, and there are many websites that can help you find events in your area. These are great opportunities to meet employers or recruiters, build up your network and learn more about the industry.

Mentors

Mentors can provide great, hands on advice and support to help guide you through choices in your career. You can find a mentor for example in your personal network, school, sports, or through mentorship programmes.

Build Your Skills

Online Training

Use online courses, just like this one, to teach yourself the skills required in your industry. There's lots to learn, and lots of places to support you in doing so.

Try Out Tools

As you learn more about Social Media, you will come across the programmes and platforms used to help Social Media professionals do their jobs. Being familiar with them and able to work with these tools is a great skill to prepare you for the job.

Start a Project

As you gain more practical and theoretical knowledge, you could start a project: maybe a blog or vlog. This is a great way to showcase your skills and gain experience in Social Media - even without an employer!

A DAY IN THE LIFE OF...
A SOCIAL MEDIA ASSISTANT

What is work in Social Media like?

If you work in Social Media, you will help to promote or represent a company on Social Media platforms to increase awareness and customer engagement.

As a Social Media Assistant, you can expect to create content for different platforms, monitor people's engagement, respond as necessary, and analyse how well previous posts have been received or what kind of content works best.

You will probably work together with a Social Media manager and help them to implement the company's Social Media marketing strategy.

As a junior Social Media professional, your entry level salary is likely to start at £18 - 23,000 a year, and rise to between £25 - 40,000 after 3-5 years in the job. These figures vary depending on your location and industry.

What are some of the key skills that you'd develop in this job?

 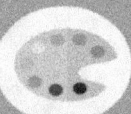   

Writing and copy-editing	Boldness & Creativity	No fear of numbers	Interest in digital & networks	Communication
You will likely write copy yourself or proofread what others have written.	In social media you have only seconds to attract attention - creating interesting hooks is key.	You will do some analysis of data to find out what works and what doesn't.	You'll want to stay on top of trends, new networks and successful campaigns.	In the end, it's all about getting your message across - in person, in writing and via multiple media.

Patrick
Social Media Manager

Patrick completed the Social Media course while still in school, where he was responsible for **promoting his school's football team on Facebook**. He had always really enjoyed that, but was excited when he realised that Social Media could be a profession! When he finished school, he wanted to start earning money straight away, so he applied for an **apprenticeship as a Social Media Assistant**.

Patrick was accepted - he would **even earn a degree** while gaining **practical work experience in a Social Media agency**. Whenever he didn't know what to do, he used **online resources** or asked for support from his more senior colleagues.

Once his apprenticeship ended, the company unfortunately couldn't make him a permanent offer, but because of his experience, he was **able to secure a new job within two months**. He loves to work across campaigns and clients, and chose to become a **"generalist"** Social Media Manager to keep his work varied.

Andrea
Social Media Community Manager

Andrea had been working in fashion retail, but her real passion was a **fashion blog** she had been writing for a while. As the number of her followers rose, she took the Social Media course to find out more about potential careers in Social Media. Her interest grew: she subscribed to Social Media **podcasts**, took **online training** and **grew her blog** across multiple platforms! She now was determined that she wanted to try a career in Social Media.

Andrea started going to **networking events** to reach out to professionals in the field and got to know a Social Media Manager who agreed to **mentor** her. The mentor helped Andrea to find **work experience as a Social Media assistant with** a large online fashion retailer who were impressed with Andrea's knowledge and her willingness to learn more, extending her work experience before making her a permanent offer.

Andrea found that what she really loved about her work was the opportunity to engage customers via Social Media and chose to **specialise** as a **Social Media Community Manager**. She's now responsible for managing the online interactions between her brand and their customers.

Tamas
Social Media Executive

Tamas had always been fascinated by the way companies use Social Media to promote their brand and interact with their customers. He had **watched numerous talks, had listened to podcasts and was following some blogs** to learn more about it, before he decided to enroll in a digital marketing course at **university**.

On his summer break, Tamas completed an **internship with a Social Media marketing agency**, who offered him a job when he graduated.

Tamas realised that what he loves about Social Media is the vast variety of work involved with the job, and the fact he can work with multiple clients. Instead of choosing to specialise, Tamas became a **"generalist"** Social Media Executive and now manages Social Media for brands in all sorts of industries.

THE END

[64]

www.ingramcontent.com/pod-product-compliance
Lightning Source LLC
Chambersburg PA
CBHW051332220526
45468CB00004B/1608